AF406838

ENVOI

Shirley Gentry

Gotham Books

30 N Gould St.
Ste. 20820, Sheridan, WY 82801
https://gothambooksinc.com/

Phone: 1 (307) 464-7800

Published by Gotham Books (June 20, 2023)

ISBN: 979-8-88775-325-6 (P)
ISBN: 979-8-88775-326-3 (E)

Because of the dynamic nature of the Internet, any web addresses or links contained in this book may have changed since publication and may no longer be valid.

The views expressed in this work are solely those of the author and do not necessarily reflect the views of the publisher, and the publisher hereby disclaims any responsibility for them.

MISSOURI

Here's a revelation
For anyone who strays.
Whatever the direction,
A road must lead two ways.

Each time I travel down the road,
Fills me with such yearning.
Every time I go away,
I wish I was returning.

There are many chances
For rovers to amend.
U-turns, ramps and cloverleafs,
Options without end.

No matter what the years may bring,
How many times that I unpack,
The road that leads away from you
Will always bring me back.

Flowers grow in isolation,
Flowers grow in tandem,
Without the help of human hands,
Flowers grow at random.

They do not choose their colors,
They do not choose their breed,
Flowers show no bias,
They'll live next to a weed.

Flowers with all their beauty,
Brighten up the day,
Although they travel daily,
Flowers get no pay.

Flowers go to funerals,
Flowers go to balls,
Flowers go to weddings,
They decorate the halls.

They help to lighten up the day,
For people on the mend,
And, they are a lovely way
To say 'Hi' to a friend.

(From a jingle)

A heart in transit roves about
without a clear direction.
It's always searching tirelessly
to make a new connection.

A floundering heart that's weary
and feeling all at sea,
a heart that has no place to go
when it has been set free.

The world it knows is on the wane
with the customs that it can't sustain
and feelings that it can't explain,
it is a heart in transit.

A knight in shining armor
awakes me with a kiss.
The little boy down in the lane
fills my life with bliss.
A strong and handsome sailor
sails upon the brine
and, even though he's out to sea,
he holds this heart of mine.
A tan and happy farmer
working in his field,
hopes for rain and sunshine,
the soil, it's fruit to yield.
To lead a full, rewarding life
He always has a flair.
A man of truth and honor—
the nicest anywhere.
All those I have mentioned
have a common name,
for you're every one of them,
you're all one in the same.

As I travel through the world,
I occupy a place.
No matter where I chance to be,
I take up some space.

And, you, no matter where you stand
at any given time.
That certain space belongs to you,
that space we all consign.

Why not bring your private space
into proximity?
Let's put our spaces into sync.
Come share your space with me.

Dear friend, although you're far from view
here are the things I wish for you:

Sunshine shedding beams of gold
to fill up your treasure trove.
Gentle rains from day to day
to wash all your cares away.
May your path be strewn with flowers,
your days be spent in leafy bowers.
Choirs of birds all twittering,
a song your heart can learn to sing.
And in the evening, rosy skies,
soft winds to sing you lullabies.
A heart that's always by your side
when you return at eventide

I see you running through the leaves
on an autumn day.
The wind has caught your flowing hair,
enhancing the ballet.

And now, you're very pensive—
completely lost in thought.
It always gives me pause to see
your face in wonder wrought.

Eating cotton candy,
swinging on a swing.
What a lot of fun we have,
biking in the spring.

You're there in all your handsomeness,
your life in every stage.
In my book of memories,
You're on every page.

At times, I am lonely,
disheartened and blue.
A feeling of yearning
that I can't subdue.

It's then I remember
a moment of bliss.
The delight that I found
in a magical kiss.

A moment to treasure,
a memory sublime.
The thought of a kiss
that is frozen in time.

Picture us together
in a garden by the sea.
You are in a hammock,
picking daisies, that is me.
Imagine pretty butterflies
of every shade and hue,
polliwogs and dragonflies
and birds to sing on cue.
Pretend that we are happy,
it's such a lovely day.
Then a sudden cloudburst
washes all of it away.

I lost my heart in London town
all on a summer's day,
I was only passing through,
I didn't mean to stay.
A light rain had begun to fall,
then I saw through the mist
a handsome, kind and smiling face
that I could not resist.
And then the sun broke through the clouds
and smiled on us below.
So, now, my heart's in London town,
it has its own rainbow.

Extraordinary is any time with you.
It doesn't seem to matter, what it is we do.
Any place I walk with you,
we're in a grand parade.
I hear you singing in the shower,
a lovely serenade.
When we two are dancing,
any setting is a ball.
It's a great excursion,
to go shopping at the mall.
You do things that make me laugh
(I'm easy to amuse).
Anything you say to me
sounds like front page news.
You fill my days with whimsy,
you fill my nights with bliss.
Extraordinary—
a trip I wouldn't miss.

Although you kiss a lot of lips
That you may soon forget,
It is the thrill of love's first kiss
That lingers with you yet.

When callow youth is on the wane
And autumn has begun,
All the boys you've loved and lost
Fade-except for one.

Even after countless springs,
There still remains an ember.
It is the one that you first loved
You always will remember.

You have something no one else has,
Something you may not know.
It is a deep, dark secret that
I want to tell you so.

I know something you can count on
That will fail you never.
You have something to depend on
That will last forever.

It isn't that you're wonderful
And gifted with esprit.
You have something no one else has,
You have me.

When you hear noises,
do you ever find,
that you get a vision
that's colored in mind?

What scary color is ,
the creak in the walls?
What color's the patter
of rain as it falls?

What color's the crash
of the waves in the bay?
What color's the force
that makes seed grow in May?

To think of a sigh
as a color is odd.
What color is laughter?
What color is God?

Where do I find you?
Where can you be?
Are you out somewhere
looking for me?
I go out searching—
but all in vain.
Instead of the sunshine
I only find rain.
Maybe tomorrow
out on the street
without a warning
we two will meet.
How will I know you?
Will you know me?
Will we just pass
like ships on the sea?
A chance lost forever
to share happiness,
to never know heaven
our union to bless.
Where do I find you?
Where can you be?
Are you out somewhere
looking for me?

Like time and the river
I go on forever
And to the beginning
We'll never return.
We all three change forms
We all three change places.
And, over the years,
we all three change faces.
Time circles the globe
and we call it a day.
The river runs happily
into the bay.
I watch my time ticking
slowly away.
Time sees the centuries
turn each anew.
The river's recycled
and turned into dew.
I search my soul
but, I haven't a clue.
Like time and the river
I go on forever.
We're all bound together,
our bonds we can't sever.

In this world where dreams come true
Or, sometimes, maybe not.
When you go out for a walk
It's either cold or hot.
In this world of lose or win
Sometimes you're out, sometimes you're in.
In this world of might have been
There is always you.

In this world where skies are blue
Unless the skies are gray.
In this world where friends are true
Unless they turn away.
In this world of joys and woes,
In this world of highs and lows,
In this world of maybe sos,
There is always you.

Am I missing something?
Don't you love me anymore?
Am I making any points
or simply keeping score?
What is this we're playing?
Does it even have a name?
Am I still a contender?
Am I even in the game?
Are we going for the countdown?
Do I get another chance?
Why can't I get lucky
in this thing they call romance?

There's such a magnetism
between us when you're near.
It is a wild phenomena
that I both love and fear.

Wherever else I chance to be
you will always own my heart.
My love will always be for you
but our worlds are far apart.

I'd like to stay and be with you
when the morning comes.
But something deep inside says, "Go"
and I hear distant drums.

The world is full of options,
Nothing's black or white.
When you come to a corner,
should you turn left or right?

You go out to a movie,
you hope it is a hit.
After you have stepped inside,
you choose a place to sit.

You make some big decisions,
when you go out to eat.
The waiter will ask you—
'Would you like white or wheat?'

When it comes to choosing someone
it's not hard to do.
There is only one to love,
that someone is you.

GOOD NIGHT, MY LOVE

Float off into the liquid night
Where all your troubles will alight.
Sail on into unconscious bliss,
Guided by an angel's kiss.
You'll find, descending from above,
All the fluff that dreams are of.
Bask in stardust, for you may,
All along the Milky Way.
Traverse all night that endless sea.
When you awake--return to me.

I've forgotten how you looked
with snowflakes in your hair
And that worn out pair of jeans
you always used to wear.

I don't remember how we loved
and laughed and, sometimes, cried
And how we shared our love and dreams,
then, somehow, our love died.

I can't recall the way you looked
the day you went away.
Didn't I call out to you
and ask you, 'Please', to stay?

If I could remember,
I would miss you so.
But that is impossible,
I forgot you long ago.

Anything in life may happen,
you may swing upon a star.
Just expect the unexpected,
it doesn't matter where you are.

Luck is just around the corner
standing, smiling right at you,
telling you your secret wishes
are no longer overdue.

You are going to be a winner,
you are destined to go far.
Anything in life may happen.
luck will find you where you are.

You are a work in progress,
outstanding piece of art,
an image by the master
with aplomb set apart.

An alabaster monument
carved with a craftsman's touch,
a graphic for the ages,
an opus creme deluxe.

When reality sets in,
we will understand what's happened.
When reality sets in,
then we will start to know.
In the solitude hereafter,
we will have some time to reason.
After we have thought it through,
we will know which way to go.

When reality sets in,
we will see the way more clearly.
When reality sets in,
we will realize our plight.
After slowly sorting through it,
then we will have the answer.
We will weigh it in the balance,
we will see it in the light.

Listen to your heart,
it will lead the way
to your own safe haven
and a brighter day.

Love can be mistaken
for a myriad of things.
Affairs that we think are real
may be only flings.

When when we think we're wise,
we're not always smart
about who wins the custody
of our trusting heart.

Listen to your heart,
for it knows what's best.
It will lead you safely home
where you, at last, may rest.

Everyone awaits tomorrow,
thinking with the coming dawn,
everything will be much better,
all their worries will be gone.

I don't think about tomorrow,
I can't let it bother me.
Today is all that I hang onto,
tomorrow may never be.

Don't depend upon the future,
the future soon is in the past.
I believe now is tomorrow.
Hold each fleeting moment fast,
try to make each moment last.

The least of all the things you are,
a measure of the norm,
the most of all the things you are,
a template of rare form.
An image that's reflected
in a constellation far.
A class act far exceeding par,
unique in all the world you are.

Any day that I can rise
and greet the morning sun
and feel a playful, gentle breeze
and watch a river run.

And I can hear the haunting strains
of a melody
that plays upon my heart strings
and sets my fancy free.

Any day that I see joy
in a loved one's eyes
or win complete approval
of a friend I prize.

Any day that I can help
someone along the way,
that's a day I'm thankful for.
Thank you for that day.

At the end of the day
we reflect on the hours
that we spend in the fray
and we spend midst the flowers.

Each morning begins
all shiny and new
with many adventures
before it is through.

A day may be cheery,
a world of delight.
It may be an ogre
that we have to fight.

Our joy's measured by
the price that we pay,
when all's said and done
at the end of the day.

I know you are out there,
I just don't know where.
Can you hear my heart calling you
or are you unaware?
Outside, the night is hollow,
inside the mood is tense.
I am lonely in a crowd,
my longing is immense.
Do you know that you are missed?
Are you aware that I exist?
Are you searching for me, too?
Forever, I will wait for you.

Nothing left for me to build a dream on.
Nothing left to tie my future to.
No way to rekindle all the plans
that once were ours.
Nothing left since I'm left without you.

Once, I thought I'd always be
welcome in your heart.
Once, I thought you'd never set me free.
But, now, you're gone and I'm left
to journey all alone.
I'm here by myself and all at sea.

Someday, down the road, I'll find a new love.
Someday, down the road, my heart will mend.
I know when it happens,
I'll know joy once more.
But, for now, I miss you so my friend.

I'll go down any road with you,
I'll tread the byways my life through.
I'll walk through blizzards, hail and fire—
any place that you desire.
No obstacle too great or small.
We will overcome them all.
No hill too high, no goal too far.
Together, we can light a star.
I'll be happy anywhere Just as long as you are there.

Tall oaks from small acorns grow,
hard to imagine-but it's so.
Nature proves that, yes, indeed
an oak tree springs from one small seed.

It is exciting when we find
one small idea in the mind
becomes something so profound
it changes our whole life around.

Because the thoughts that we elect
may have a far-reaching effect,
may all of our ideas be
as lofty as that mighty tree.

(First line from an old saying)

The heaven opened up tonight
and sent a calming rain,
and it defused all tensions
with its resolute refrain.

Now and then, up in the sky,
a 'fiery display.
Whatever cares were on my mind,
completely washed away.

While the gray clouds cover
the ever-constant moon,
raindrops, with their steady beat,
remind the world's in tune.

This is your final notice,
remit by return mail.
Send back the heart you took from me
and do it without fail.
Return in mint condition,
a penalty if late.
And this is very crucial—
don't bend or mutilate.

Your true love tells you au revoir,
the G string breaks on your guitar,
an uninsured guy hits your car
but every now and then, you win one.

Some mornings you don't feel so spry,
your ready funds have all run dry,
the world just seems to pass you by
but every now then, you win one.

Your favorite team just lost again,
you have to take it on the chin,
you know your ship will not come in
but every now and then, you win one.

Sometimes now, I get confused
and don't know if I put
my shirt tag in the 'front or back,
or, which shoe on which foot.

Sometimes I go downtown
because I have some bills to pay.
Secretaries tell me that
I paid them yesterday.

I can't find my glasses,
I'm convinced they're gone.
When I look into the mirror,
I see I have them on.

Sometimes little usual things
catch me way off guard.
The things I used to do with ease
now seem so darned hard.

Be patient with me, lass and lad.
Forgive the things I do.
For, in the twinkling of an eye,
this fate will befall you.

Adam was a lonely man
so God gave him a mate.
A spouse in female form named Eve
whom the serpent used for bait.

The snake gave Eve an apple
which was forbidden fruit.
She passed it on to Adam,
he then put on a suit.

Remember, when you're lonely
and you are feeling glib,
be careful what you ask for.
It might cost you a rib.

Word, words. words, words,
For everything and places,
And, they always match
With the expressions on our faces.
Sometimes we wear a smiley face,
And, say "How do you do?"
Sometimes we wear a grinchy face
That says, "The same to you."
In church we wear angelic looks,
Pretend that we don't sin
And, when the sermon's over,
We all say, "Amen."

I have a special happy face
That I reserve for you
And, I can say with certainty,
"I really mean it, too."

Bells ring softly in a distance.
Everything seems bright and new.
The sun beams down in all its glory.
Grass is gleaming, wet with dew.

Flowers spread a mild aroma,
Lending aura to the scene,
And their colors render contrast
To a world that is turning green.

Buds awaiting to burst open,
All the earth's reborn.
Joy exudes from out the welkin
On a beauteous Easter morn.

I will always carry
the memory of your smile.
You radiated sunshine,
you made my life worthwhile.

You brought a new dimension
to my world of commonplace.
It always gave me solace
to look into your face.

You were a dear companion,
you were there day and night.
I knew I could depend on you.
you were my heart's delight.

I offer you an olive branch
delivered by a dove.
To you, wherever you may be—
forever, peace and love.

I came to talk to you today
to tell you everything's okay.
Here upon a windy hill
where you lie so calm and still
beneath your clover coverlet
I can feel your presence yet.
Every day I miss you so—
I just thought that you should know
that's the reason that I came.
Nothing's ever been the same.
I came to talk to you today
to tell you everything's okay.

Leaves, many times, have turned from green
to withered shades of brown.
Summer skies have given way
to snowflakes drifting down.

Hours slip by slowly, one by one,
as sands in an hourglass.
Only a lonely heart can know
how slowly time can pass.

Many days have melded into
an eternity.
Many nights have now gone by
since you were here with me.

A full moon shines
on strange demonics.
Shadows move
enhanced bionics.

Hoots and howls
pierce the air.
Barks and growls
enough to scare.

Children morphed
into strange creatures.
Masks conceal
their childish features.

Ghosts and ghouls
with paper sacks,
eagerly await
some snacks.

Reality exists between
a plethora of things unseen.
But, then, of course,
it's Halloween.

I don't mind spiders,
I think they're alright.
And slithery snakes
never get me uptight.
Cute little mice
don't set me in flight.

The things that I dread—
that give me a fright
are all of those things
that go bump in the night.

Things have changed since you've been gone.
The tree out on the hill
has shed its final golden leaves,
its nestling birds are still.

The house is boarded up and locked,
the key's under the mat.
The grass has covered up the spot
where the gazebo sat.

Perhaps someday, a youth will see
his future there-and then,
he'll rebuild a home with love,
the land will live again.

The Pilgrims and the Indians
sat down to eat together
the fall of 1621,
before the cold, cold weather.

Their meal was very similar
to what we eat today.
But they ate many kinds of fish,
for they lived by the bay.

They ate turkey, which was wild,
and crops that they had grown.
They garnered winter's store,
from seeds that they had sown.

Now, we gather in the fall
to share fruits of our labor,
with other people that we love,
the summer's yield to savor.

I crept outside one frosty morn,
my breath hung in the air.
wearing my robe and slippers
with curlers in my hair.

I opened up the mailbox,
stuffed with ads and unpaid bills
and magazines that promised
to cure all my ills.

Near the bottom of the stack,
my hands with numbness fraught,
I found a lovely Christmas card
bearing a lovely thought.

One fall day when I arose,
I found my window painted white.
Jack Frost had stolen into town
and plied his paintbrush in the night.

I found that rascal waiting
just beyond my door.
I said, "I'm still in summer mode,
What did you do that for?"

And, then, I chided further
in discordant tones quite surly,
"You are not welcome here, my friend,
because you are too early."

"I want to go outside today
without my winter clothes."
First, he laughed—then he winked
and, then, he nipped my nose.

A stranger stands outside our door,
he never will come in.
He's been there for a week or two,
he's starting to look thin.

He looks quite familiar,
we've seen him there before.
He will disappear again
and, then, come back once more.

He has been such a delight,
we have enjoyed his stay.
Although we hate to see him go,
he's bound to go away.

Inside, we are safe and warm,
he's outside standing guard.
Our current winter visitor,
the snowman in our yard.

Happy, happy birthday!
Add a candle on the cake.
If we add another one,
how many will that make?
Look at all the presents!
A horse shoe for your door,
four-leaf clover, lucky penny,
and some things you'll want to store.

Happy, happy birthday!
A day that's just for you.
After three or four of them,
they seem like deja vu.
But this birthday's special,
it's going to be a coup.
And the reason is because,
we're all here with you.

We don't know how many,
but who's keeping score?
Here's to health-here's to wealth,
and here's to many more.

REFLECTIONS ON MY 86TH BIRTHDAY

Many miles of the toil and sweat,
many blunders to regret.
Many weeds that grow and grow;
many miles of piled-up snow.
Lots of miles of smiles and tears,
raising children through the years.
Lots of joys despite the weather,
when we all could get together.
Lots of friends that I still treasure,
they were faithful without measure.
Miles of roads, new worlds to find,
missing those I left behind.

I still have some oats to sow,
a few more miles left, yet, to go.

(Bows to Robert Frost)

ON MY 88TH BIRTHDAY

Wistful child of distant yore,
heedless of what lies before:

Wonders that make your heart sing,
watching snows melt into spring.
There will be both joy and strife,
every season of your life.
You will bow when life demands.
You will walk in foreign lands.
You'll succeed when your star gleams.
Fate will buffet a few dreams.

When you look around the bend
and, see you're coming to the end—
we'll heave a contented sigh.
We're wayfarers, you and I